MAPS

Pebble®

What Is a Map?

by
Jennifer M. Besel

Consulting editor:
Gail Saunders-Smith, PhD

Consultant:
Dr. Sarah E. Battersby
Department of Geography
University of South Carolina

T0052454

CAPSTONE PRESS
a capstone imprint

Pebble Books are published by Capstone Press,
1710 Roe Crest Drive, North Mankato, Minnesota 56003
www.capstonepub.com

Copyright © 2014 by Capstone Press, a Capstone imprint. All rights reserved.
No part of this publication may be reproduced in whole or in part, or stored in a retrieval system, or transmitted in any form or by any means, electronic, mechanical, photocopying, recording, or otherwise, without written permission of the publisher.

Library of Congress Cataloging-in-Publication Data
Besel, Jennifer M.
What is a map? / by Jennifer M. Besel.
pages cm—(Pebble Books. Maps)
Includes bibliographical references and index.
Summary: "Simple text with full-color photos and illustrations provide basic information about maps"—Provided by publisher.
ISBN 978-1-4765-3081-9 (library binding)—ISBN 978-1-4765-3503-6 (ebook pdf)—
ISBN 978-1-4765-3521-0 (paperback)
1. Maps—Juvenile literature. I. Title.
GA105.6.B48 2014
912—dc23 2012046454

Editorial Credits
Gene Bentdahl, designer; Kathy McColley, production specialist; Sarah Schuette, photo stylist; Marcy Morin, scheduler

Photo Credits
Capstone: 9, 11, 13, 15; Capstone Studio: Karon Dubke, cover, 1, 5, 7, 17, 19, 21

Note to Parents and Teachers

The Maps set supports social studies standards related to people, places, and environments. This book describes and illustrates maps. The images support early readers in understanding the text. The repetition of words and phrases helps early readers learn new words. This book also introduces early readers to subject-specific vocabulary words, which are defined in the Glossary section. Early readers may need assistance to read some words and to use the Table of Contents, Glossary, Read More, Internet Sites, and Index sections of the book.

Printed in the United States 5756

MAPS

Table of Contents

Finding Your Way 4
Map Features 10
Using Maps 16

Glossary 22
Read More 23
Internet Sites 23
Critical Thinking Using the Common Core . . . 24
Index 24

Finding Your Way

Imagine you're on
a family trip. Oh, no!
You missed the turn.
Which way should you go?
Grab a map!

Maps are tools
that help you find your way.
Maps and globes show
what the world looks like
from above.

Every map shows an area of Earth. Some maps show streets and buildings. Other maps show mountains and lakes.

State Park
Star Lake
N
W
E
S
0
50 feet
15 meters
Key
Mountain
Hill
River

Map Features

All maps have a compass rose. The compass rose shows which direction is north, south, east, or west.

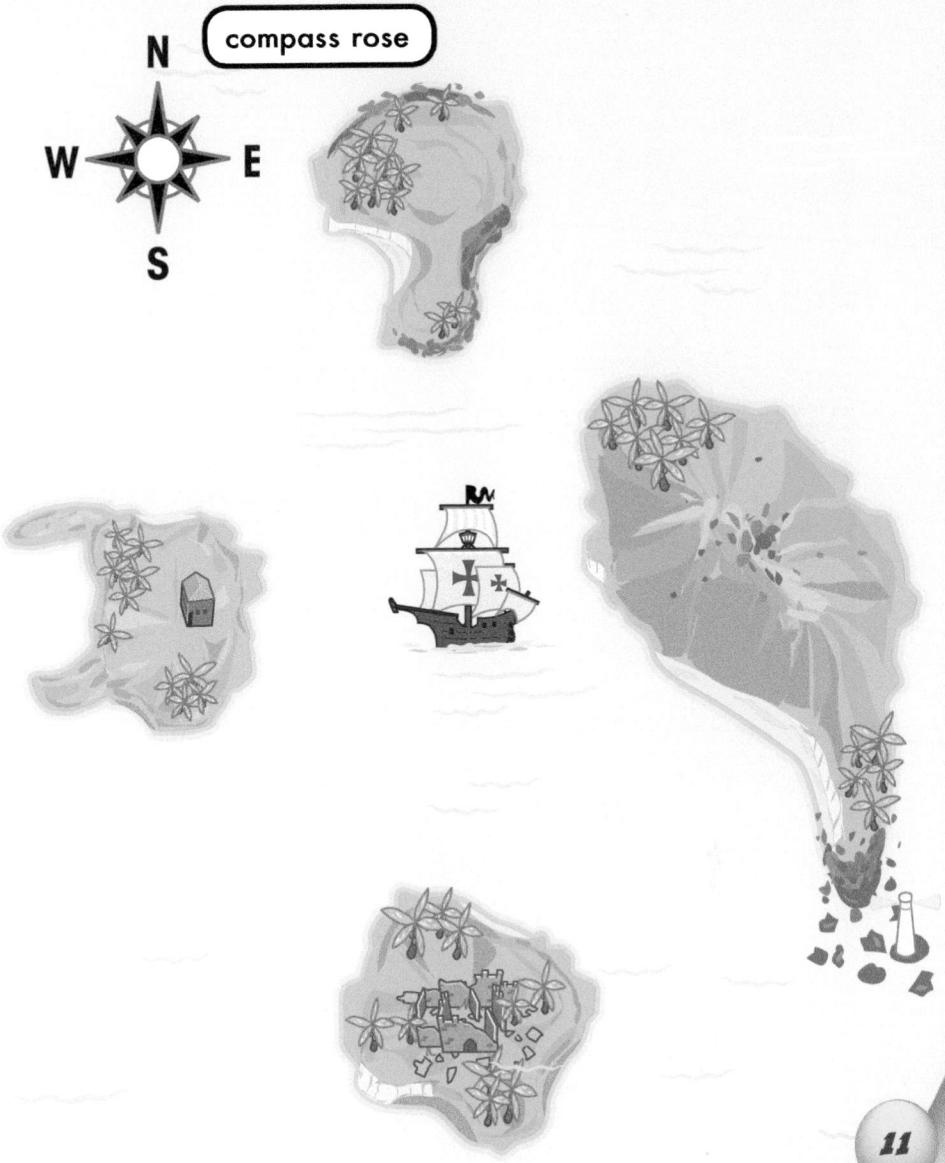
compass rose
N
W
E
S

Map symbols

stand for real places.

A blue line stands for a river.

Look at the key to see

what the symbols mean.

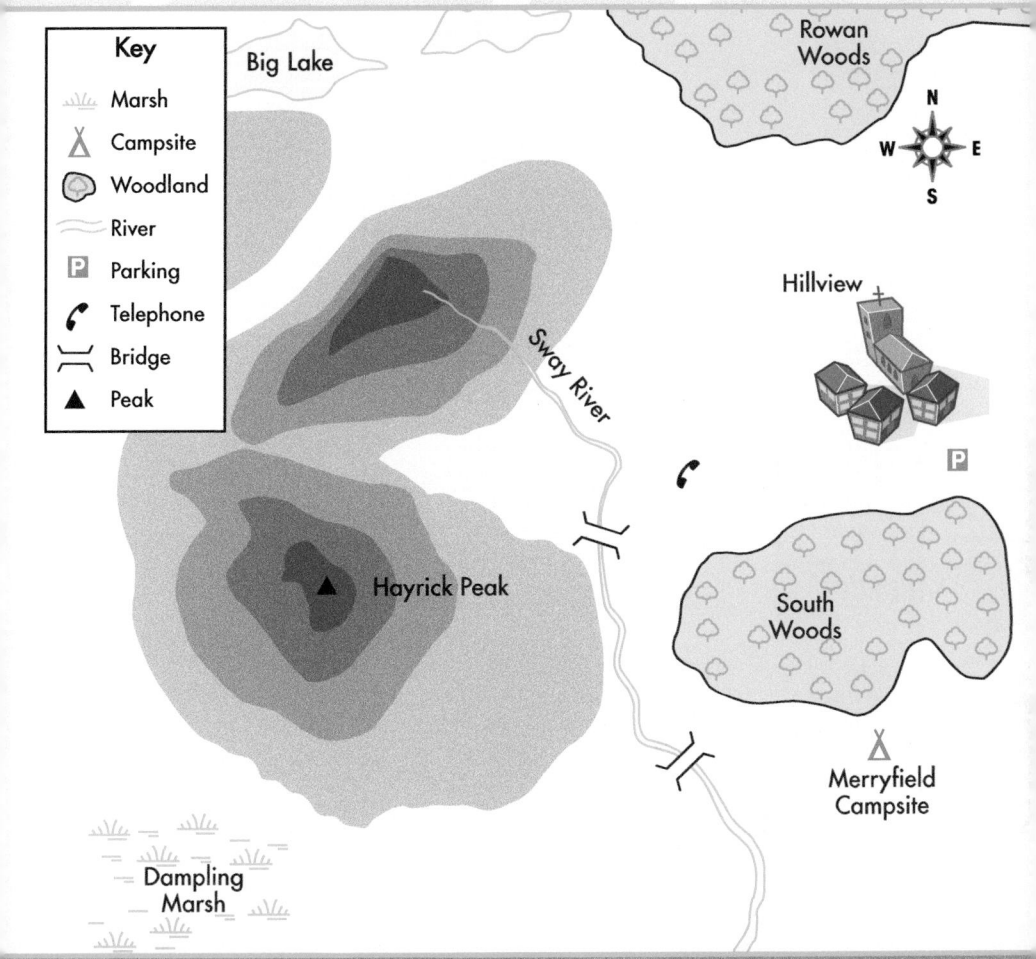
Key
Marsh
Campsite
Woodland
River
Parking
Telephone
Bridge
Peak
Big Lake
Rowan Woods
N
W
E
S
Hillview
Sway River
Hayrick Peak
South Woods
Merryfield Campsite
Dampling Marsh

Places are drawn small enough to fit on a map. A map scale tells you what a distance on the map equals on Earth.

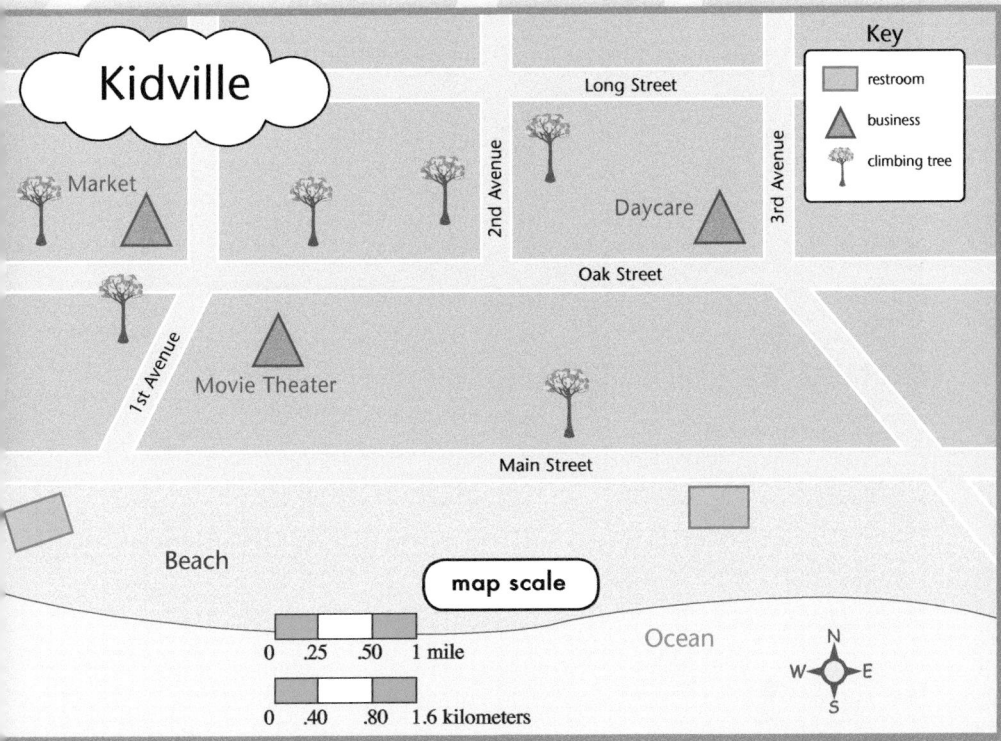
Kidville
Key
restroom
business
climbing tree
Long Street
Market
2nd Avenue
Daycare
3rd Avenue
Oak Street
1st Avenue
Movie Theater
Main Street
Beach
map scale
0 .25 .50 1 mile
0 .40 .80 1.6 kilometers
Ocean
N
W
E
S

Using Maps

People have used maps
for thousands of years.
Many old maps show
the routes ships used to get
from one place to another.

GÉOGRAPHIE primitive DES GRECS.
HÉSIODE, HOMÈRE, ORPHÉE,
neuf siècles avant notre ère.
VOYAGES DES ARGONAUTES
ET D' ULYSSE.
OCÉAN
FLEUVE
CÔTÉ DE LA NUIT (ΠΡΟΣ ΖΟΦΟΝ Homer)
plus tard EUROPE
Cimmerii
Scythæ
THRACIA
Cicones
Solymi
LIBYA
Lotophagi
ÆGYPTUS
Ethiopes
CÔTÉ DU JOUR (ΠΡΟΣ ΗΟΥ' ΗΑΛΟΝΤΕ Homer)
plus tard ASIE
Pygmæi
Pygmæi
ETHIOPIENS
ETHIOPIENS
OCCIDENTAUX
ORIENTAUX
OCÉAN
SYSTÈME DE DÉMOCRITE
IVe Siècle avant notre ère
EUROPA
LIBYA
SYSTÈME DE SCYLAX D'EUDOXE ET D'ÉPHORE
IVe et Ve Siècles avant notre ère
EUROPA
LIBYA
ASIA

Today maps are made with computers. GPS systems show maps of where you are and maps of where you are going.

VOL
SETUP
Raintree Rd
Dest
Options
Gree Ct
Gree Point Dr
Shiloh Ct
Dublin Ct
Dublin Rd
Elwin Rd
60
P10067
SECURITY
PASSENGER
AIR BAG
OFF
ON
FRONT
A/C
HI
OFF
MAX
A/C

There's a map for

almost every place on Earth.

Use a map, and you can

always find your way!

Grand Canyon
National Park
NORTH
CANYON

Glossary

compass rose—a label that shows direction on a map

direction—the way that someone or something is moving or pointing

globe—a round model of the world

GPS—an electronic tool used to find the location of an object; GPS stands for global positioning system

key—a list or chart that explains symbols on a map or graph

route—the regular path you follow to go somewhere

scale—a map tool that compares distances on a map to real distances on Earth

symbol—an object that stands for something else

Read More

Besel, Jennifer M. *Types of Maps.* Maps. Mankato, Minn.: Capstone Press, 2014.

Greve, Meg. *Maps Are Flat, Globes Are Round.* Little World Geography. Vero Beach, Fla.: Rourke Pub., 2010.

Spilsbury, Louise. *Mapping.* Investigate. Chicago: Heinemann Library, 2010.

Internet Sites

FactHound offers a safe, fun way to find Internet sites related to this book. All of the sites on FactHound have been researched by our staff.

Here's all you do:

Visit *www.facthound.com*

Type in this code: 9781476530819

Check out projects, games and lots more at
www.capstonekids.com

Critical Thinking Using the Common Core

1. Describe the features found on every map. What purpose does each feature serve? (Craft and Structure)
2. Map symbols stand for real places. What are some different meanings for the words "stand for?" (Craft and Structure)
3. Compare the maps on pages 17 and 19. Even though one map is very old and the other is new, what similarities do these maps have? Do you think that most maps have things in common, regardless of age? If so, why? If not, why not? (Craft and Structure)

Index

buildings, 8

compass roses, 10

directions, 10
distances, 14

Earth, 8, 14, 20

globes, 6
GPS systems, 18

keys, 12

lakes, 8

mountains, 8

scales, 14
ships, 16
streets, 8
symbols, 12

Word Count: 181
Grade: 1
Early-Intervention Level: 17